The Orangutan

Forest Acrobat

text by Christine Sourd
photos by Albert Visage and
Jean-Paul Ferrero/ PHO.N.E.

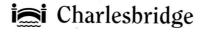 Charlesbridge

Library of Congress Cataloging-in-Publication Data
Sourd, Christine
 [Orang-outan. English]
 The orangutan: forest acrobat / Christine Sourd.
  p.   cm.—(Animal close-ups)
 Includes bibliographical references (p.).
 ISBN 1-57091-429-X (softcover)
 1. Orangutan—Juvenile literature. [1. Orangutan.] I. Title. II.
Series.
 QL737.P96 S5913 2001
 599.88'3—dc21   00-063891

Copyright © 2001 by Éditions Milan under the title *l'orang-outan, acrobate des forêts*
300 rue Léon-Joulin, 31101 Toulouse Cedex 100, France
French series editor, Valérie Tracqui

Published by Charlesbridge Publishing, 85 Main Street, Watertown, MA 02472
(617) 926-0329 • www.charlesbridge.com

The orangutan is the largest animal in the world that lives
most of its life in trees.

The orangutan lives only in the dense, humid forests of Sumatra and Borneo, two islands in Southeast Asia.

In the jungle

At noon the sun is high in the sky, but only a little light penetrates the tropical forest. It is hot and very humid.

More than fifty feet from the ground, a large ball of red fur stretches one arm out of its nest. It is an orangutan waking up from a short nap. Each day, the orangutan leaves its nest to look for food, then returns to the trees to sleep. Its territory covers up to four square miles of swamps, jungles, and hills.

Forest acrobat

The orangutan is slow and awkward on the ground because of its short legs and long arms, but it is an expert at life in the high trees. Vines and small branches become bridges, and tree trunks become ladders, allowing the orangutan to move easily through the thick jungle.

The orangutan spends most of its time eating and sleeping. It may travel only about three miles all day. Although the orangutan can move quickly, it carefully tests each branch before letting go of the one before. A fall could be deadly.

The orangutan is very acrobatic. It can hang easily from its hands or its feet.

If a branch breaks beneath the orangutan's feet, it simply grabs another branch with its long, powerful arms.

The orangutan is a bad swimmer. If it must cross a river, it often picks up
a stick to test the depth of the water.

A big, red ape

The orangutan's arms hang down to its ankles, and its feet look like a pair of hands. Rusty red fur grows all over its body, but the skin underneath looks blue, except for a small area of brown around the eyes. The orangutan has a long, jutting jaw and tiny ears. Females grow up to three and a half feet tall and weigh about eighty pounds. Males are more than twice as heavy, though they are usually only a foot taller.

The orangutan's hands and feet look the same.

The orangutan has flexible lips like a human's. This one is eating the sweet, soft pulp of a fruit.

Female orangutans and their young look almost human with their small, flat noses and shining black eyes.

The orangutan has a big toe on each foot that is separate from the rest, like a thumb. This toe allows the orangutan to use its feet like hands.

Out in the open the orangutan's rusty fur is easy to spot, but in the dark shadows of the forest these apes can be hard to find. The female talks to her baby with soft sucking sounds that will not give away their hiding place. The male, however, is territorial, and he defends his home range loudly. A vocal sack under the male's neck and rolls of fat on either side of his head help to make his calls even louder.

All males have rolls of fat on their cheeks, but only dominant males' fat rolls grow really large.

Younger males often practice screaming, but they do not have territory of their own to defend, and without large cheek rolls, their voices do not carry very far.

Finding a mate

Every now and then, the male orangutan makes a low rumbling noise that soon becomes a piercing roar and trails off in a sigh. Attracted by the call, a female moves toward the sound. The male calls again and approaches as soon as he sees the female.

The orangutans mate in the trees, sometimes fifty feet above the ground. The couple may travel together for a few days and mate often, but they never stay together very long.

Males usually avoid one another. If two males meet, they chase and threaten each other, shaking the branches violently.

Time for bed

When the sun begins to set, the orangutan carefully chooses a fork in the tree where it will sleep that night. It weaves vines and branches together and covers them with leaves. In just a few minutes, the orangutan has made a comfortable nest. The orangutan curls up in a ball and sleeps at the bottom.

In the morning, the mist rises slowly. The orangutan leaves its nest after the sun is fully up and the dew on the leaves has dried.

The orangutan builds a new nest every night.

The orangutan's long teeth help it to strip bark from tree trunks and large branches.

Its strong jaws easily break off nut shells, fruit rinds, and tough sticks.

The orangutan hides in a tree during rainstorms. Some orangutans even hold big leaves over their heads like umbrellas.

Greedy for fruit

The orangutan has favorite trees for sleeping in, favorite lookouts, and favorite places to cross rivers. Fruit is the orangutan's favorite food, but it also eats leaves, tree bark, mushrooms, insects, eggs, shellfish, and even small animals if it can find them.

For the orangutan, a fruit tree is a banquet. Its favorite is the durian, a yellow, spiny fruit about the size of a football that is said to taste like butter-almond ice cream. The orangutan may travel great distances to feast on its favorite food.

When fruit is hard to find, the orangutan eats leaves, bark, and even insects.

A newborn orangutan cannot move around by itself. It stays close to its mother until it is about a year old.

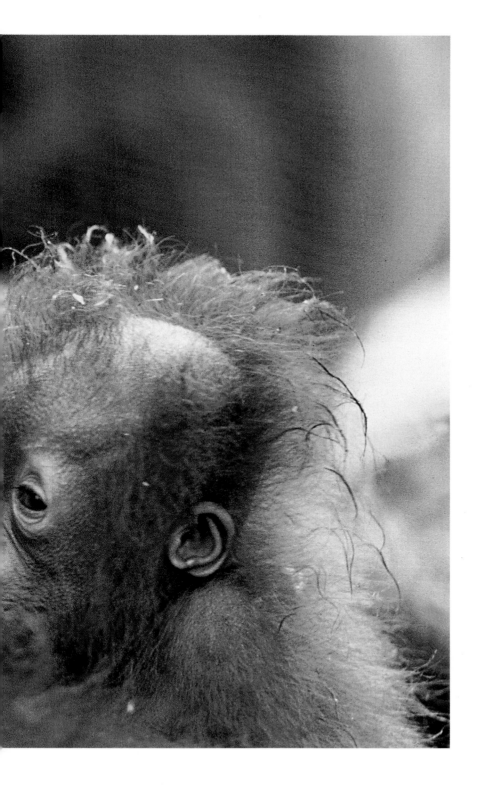

A new arrival

Eight months after mating, the female orangutan climbs into her leaf nest to give birth. The tiny baby weighs only about two pounds. Its mother shelters her newborn from the sun's harsh rays and cleans its fur with her teeth or even with rainwater. For the first few months, the mother feeds her baby milk as well as plants that she has chewed to a fine paste.

During the day, the baby travels safely in its mother's arms. At night, it sleeps next to her in her nest. After a few weeks, the baby learns to hold on to its mother's fur when she moves around.

An active childhood

When it is about a year old, the baby orangutan begins to eat fruit as well as milk and chewed plants. Its mother encourages it to hang on to branches instead of her fur, but the baby is still very clumsy. Learning to walk and climb high in the trees is dangerous. If the baby falls, it could die.

When the little orangutan is about three or four years old, it begins to make its own nest. At first this is just a game, but soon the young orangutan spends every night alone, though never very far away from its mother.

This orangutan mother carries her baby on her head so that it won't get wet when she crosses a deep river.

The mother orangutan walks on all fours on the ground. Her baby must hang on tight!

This baby finds some delicious leaves to eat.

Baby orangutans make an easy meal for pythons.

The young orangutan is very flexible. It loves to hang off a tree branch and stretch out its body.

The great pied hornbill competes with the orangutan for figs, which both animals like to eat.

A three-year-old orangutan knows how to feed itself. It uses its teeth and hands to pull leaves and fruit from the trees.

A party

The orangutan can remember which trees bear fruit each season. Every so often, several orangutan mothers bring their babies to the same tree. The adults ignore each other, but the young orangutans are happy to play together. They jump up and down, chew each other's fur, and chase one another for hours.

Gibbons, another kind of primate, also like to eat fruit and often show up at an orangutan feast. The two groups munch peacefully side by side. There is enough fruit for everyone.

Two families find the same fruit tree. The young orangutans get to play with others their age for the first time.

Growing up

The young orangutan stays with its mother until it is about eight years old, even if she has another baby. When an orangutan is ready to live independently, it joins a group of other young orangutans for a while before striking out on its own.

A male orangutan is ready to mate at age ten, but females seem to prefer older mates, so males may have to wait until they are fifteen years old. A female often has her first baby when she is seven to ten years old. She has a new baby every four or five years and spends the rest of her life protecting her babies from the dangers of the jungle.

Young orangutans are very vulnerable. Four out of every ten babies die before reaching adulthood.

Our close cousins

Orangutan is a Malaysian word meaning "man of the forest." Even though the orangutan is closely related to humans, this intelligent animal is now almost extinct. Only about 20,000 wild orangutans survive in Borneo and Sumatra. People cut down more forests each year, and hunters still kill many females and sell their babies as pets. Wildlife rescue centers tirelessly help return captive orangutans to life in the wild.

Orangutans are cute when they are young, but an adult orangutan is too dangerous to be a pet.

A sad history

For thousands of years, people hunted the orangutan for food. These apes were eventually wiped out in Java. Over the last one hundred years, thousands of young orangutans have been caught and sent to European and American zoos. Many died on the trip or soon after their arrival.

In 1960, Malaysia and Indonesia passed laws protecting orangutans, and in 1977, the international trade in orangutans was banned. Only babies born in captivity can be sold legally to research facilities or exchanged between zoos.

Unfortunately, the baby orangutan trade will never fully end as long as people still want them as pets. Tame and gentle while young, adult orangutans often have to be caged or taken by the authorities. Rehabilitation centers work to teach orangutans how to live in the wild, but few captive orangutans succeed in learning how to live on their own again.

For more than twenty years, Biruté Galdikas has taught orphaned orangutans how to live on their own in the forest.

No forest means no orangutans

The biggest threat to wild orangutans is the destruction of their forest homes. Pulp and paper mills and loggers transform thousands of square miles of jungle into cocoa or palm oil plantations, where apes can no longer live. Only a few orangutans are safe in national parks and nature preserves. The others watch helplessly as more of their territory disappears every day.

Returning to the wild

When orphaned orangutans arrive at a wildlife center, they are quarantined so that they cannot spread infection and disease. If the orangutans are healthy, wildlife conservationists release them in small groups into areas where wild orangutans live. It is hard to readjust to life in the forest. Captive orangutans are dependent on people and do not know how to find food, climb trees, build nests, or hide from predators. Wild orangutans may chase the newcomers away from their territories or even kill them. Many released orangutans come back to the wildlife centers for food and safety.

Wildlife conservationists feed orphaned orangutans bottled milk and fruit picked by people until the orphans learn to find their own food.

African cousins

The orangutan is part of the Pongidae, or great ape, family. It is the only ape that still lives in Asia. All the rest live in Africa. The great apes do not have a tail. Their bodies are covered in short hair, but their faces and ears are almost hairless. Their arms are longer than their legs, and the second finger of each hand is long while the thumb is short. All great apes have a big toe separated from the rest on each foot, making their feet look like hands. Like humans, the great apes are very intelligent. Many captive apes have learned to communicate with their keepers using sign language.

The *chimpanzee* is a real clown. It mimics all kinds of sounds and loves to scream. The chimpanzee is a little bigger, lighter, and livelier than the orangutan. It climbs trees easily, but also moves quickly on the ground. The chimpanzee lives in a big family group in humid forests and tree-filled savannas. It eats fruit, insects, and small animals.

The *gorilla* is a peaceful giant. It is the biggest of the great apes, but it is usually gentle and calm. An adult male is as tall as a human and often has silver fur on his back. The gorilla is extremely strong. It moves around the forest floor all day looking for twigs, bark, leaves, and ferns to eat. At night, it builds a nest of branches on the ground.

◄ The *bonobo*, or *pygmy chimpanzee*, lives near the Zaire River. It has a very narrow body and long legs, and it is thinner than the common chimpanzee. The bonobo moves easily on the ground and through the trees. Small families of six to fifteen bonobos travel through the forest looking for fruit, leaves, and new shoots to eat.

For Further Reading on Orangutans . . .

Cherry, Lynne. <u>First Wonders of Nature: Orangutan</u>. Dutton Children's Books, 1998.

Gallardo, Evelyn. <u>Among the Orangutans: The Biruté Galdikas Story</u>. Chronicle Books, 1993.

Levine, Stuart P. <u>The Orangutan</u>. Lucent Books, 1999.

Woods, Mae. <u>Orangutans</u>. Abdo & Daughters, 1998.

To See Orangutans in Captivity . . .

Folzenlogen, Darcy and Robert. <u>The Guide to American Zoos and Aquariums</u>.
  Willow Press, 1993.

Many zoos also have web sites on the Internet. To learn more about their exhibits, go to the following page on the Yahoo web site:

http://dir.yahoo.com/Science/Biology/Zoology/Zoos

Use the Internet to Find Out More about Orangutans and Other Great Apes. . . .

The Orangutan Foundation International
—Find out just how smart orangutans are! Read fun facts and learn how you can help scientists save the orangutan.
   http://www.orangutan.org/index.htm

Orangutan Facts
—See photos and a map showing where orangutans live, participate in a foster program, and learn all about orangutan life.
   http://www.ns.net/orangutan/facts.html

Rainforest Action Network
—Learn what you can do to help orangutans survive in the wild.
   http://www.ran.org/kids_action/index.html